The TRUTH is in HERE

"The author's humor really made me laugh out loud or maybe my sense of humor is just up for a witty remark. Whichever it is I enjoyed reading this short, but self-explanatory essay on Freemasonry. It even managed to teach me an odd bit of history or two."

"This is an excellent little introduction to the world of Freemasonry. Made me smile at a couple of bits as the guy is quite funny."

"I know a couple of hardcore conspiracy theorists, and I've always suspected they were full-blown nuts. I no longer have to suspect that, now I know it's true."

"It's a prime example of why I continue to tell people that Bernard Schaffer is a writer to watch and a brilliant essayist."

Regarding FREEMASONRY

Everything You Wanted to Know About Masonic Conspiracies, Illuminati, and More

Bernard Schaffer

CONTENTS

Author's Note

1: Regarding Freemasonry

2: Proof of a Conspiracy! Or, Something Close to It

3: An Incomplete but Still Thoroughly Engaging List of People Who Were Freemasons

4: The Internet, or, Affirmations for Silly People

5: Which Brings Us to Jack the Ripper

6: Somewhere, a Whole Lot of Villages Are Missing Their Idiots

7: But Wait, It Gets Better

8: Blame It All On Albert Pike (I Do)

9: And With All That Said, Something IS Rotten in Denmark

10: Questions and Answers

About the Author

Copyright

Author's Note

The internet has brought us many wonderful things, including an unprecedented ease of access to information. The unfortunate side effect of that is the plethora of false information and straight up falsehood.

This book is intended to be a whimsical examination of some of those lies and my attempt to set the record straight. Some readers have swallowed the bull so completely they are not able to think clearly enough to understand anything other than "The Illuminati runs the planet" and "New World Order" slogans.

I hope, if that is your mindset, you keep reading.

Chapter 1: Regarding Freemasonry

My interest in Freemasonry began as I became serious about studying the history of the United States of America. It is impossible to truly examine our beginnings as a nation and not see the Masonic influence over the men who founded it. The mark of Freemasonry can be found etched into our national monuments, hidden in the design of our currency, and intertwined into the very documents that birthed this country.

Much has been made of that. Some of it was actually correct.

Most of what is written today about Freemasons are conspiracy theories shouting about "New World Orders" and other inaccuracies inspired by fiction. I've watched the same re-enactments you have on the History Channel of "secret Masonic rituals," and I can tell you this much: I don't know what those folks were up to, but it sure did look like fun.

Right? All the masks and robes and stuff? Pretty cool.

I am a Freemason. A brief listing of my pedigree would read: Master Mason in a Blue Lodge, Royal Arch Master Mason and Knight Templar.

Getting in was simple. I applied to each of those various organizations and paid the required dues to show up a few nights and go through the initiation proceedings. That's the big mystery. That's how hard it was to do it.

No one in my family has ever been a Freemason before. My father said he was interested in joining many years ago, but could not afford the dues. Coming from a long-line of blue collar workers with large families, I'm not surprised that I'm the first to be able to afford it.

Initially, I had no idea how to become a Freemason. All I knew was that the myths about them both intrigued and entranced me. In short, I wanted to see what went on behind those closed doors, and there's only one way to find out. So I did.

The old adage of Freemasons is that "To Be One, Ask One."

I'll consider your interest in this book as you're asking me, but if you tell anybody I replied, a secret team of ninja assassins will come to your house and kill all your goldfish using an ancient dagger from the mines of King Solomon.

Just kidding.

I showed up on my very first night at the Masonic Lodge after a long, long application process. The Lodge can only do so many First Degrees at any given time, so if there are a lot of applicants, your wait can stretch on for months. Mine did.

But finally, it was the night, and I was there on time. Alone. There was nobody else around.

I walked through the Lodge, looking for people, but saw no one. Finally, I ventured up the steps and saw two closed doors. There were voices inside.

Whoever was supposed to be sitting outside of the doors was not there that night (might have been in the bathroom. He's an old guy.) so I sat on the bench and waited.

That's when my mind began to play tricks on me. Was I supposed to knock on the door? Were they waiting for me to show them how serious I was about being a member? Was this all part of some test?

I got up to go knock, then changed my mind and sat back down. What if I was just supposed to wait? What if it was like the scene from Fight Club where you just had to keep showing up and standing outside of the door patiently until someone finally took pity on you and allowed you inside?

So I waited. And waited. And that's when my imagination started to run wild.

What really was about to go on? I was putting myself at the mercy of an entire room of men who, for all I knew, secretly ran the world and engaged in animal sacrifice.

I comforted myself by thinking that whatever was about to take place inside of that room had been in existence for centuries. Whatever the ritual or ceremony I was about to partake in, it would be much the same as the one George

Washington underwent. For me, taking a step into Freemasonry was the equivalent of taking a step into history, to hear the things the great men of our country heard and said.

Finally someone did come out and ask me if I was ready.

I told them that I was. I was escorted to a small room and instructed on how to go about preparing to enter the Lodge of Freemasons for the first time. It's something you never forget. When you are going into closed rooms with no idea of what is inside waiting for you, no clue about what the people intend to do, it requires a certain measure of trust.

Trust in people you've never met.

Trust in the people you've admired throughout history.

I kept telling myself that whatever happened to me had happened to things greater than I for countless years, and somehow, it made every step I took that much easier.

It is, by far, easier to tell you what Freemasonry is not, than what it actually *is*. First of all, it is not a religion. There is no specific religious instruction, and no claim of any particular deity.

This seems to be a sticking point for the religious organizations who disavow Freemasonry. They get angry because THEIR God isn't singled out as the real one. I personally see this as a traditional practice of non-discrimination. If any church wants to tell me that's a sin, so be it, but they do it with the air of prejudice against everyone outside of their particular denomination.

The Freemasons are not a religious organization, so it really does not matter what the individual member's particular belief is. It never becomes an issue, because it is never brought up.

I realize that's hard for people to wrap their heads around. It was for me as well, because I initially thought the Masons had their own religion. They don't.

The only Masonic requirement in terms of religion is that you as a person accept the existence of God. Whether that means the Christian, Jewish, Islamic, or Glycon the make-believe Roman snake deity, they don't say. It isn't asked. Whatever God you take with you into Freemasonry is the one they are talking about.

Freemasonry is not a cult. It is also not a political organization. There has never once been, in my experience, any effort to rally the brethren to partake in any political event. There was no mention of any Presidential Elections, no support offered by the body to any candidate, and no Freemason representation at any of the voting polls.

If anything, there are more rules against what can be discussed inside of the Lodge that prevent people from talking about religion and politics than any kind of encouragement to do so.

There is no central leadership of Freemasonry outside that of the state any lodge operates in.

I'm going to say this again, because it is a fundamental point when we discuss conspiracy theories that the Freemasons are attempting to take over the world.

There is NO central leadership of Freemasonry outside of the state any lodge operates in.

Pennsylvania's Grand Lodge is located in Philadelphia. It has no connection to the Grand Lodge of New Jersey, California, London, Nova Scotia, or anywhere else. Everybody in other parts of the country and world might do things completely different than we do, and that's okay, because there is no governing body between the two.

If you are a Freemason reading this thinking, "This guy's nuts, that's not how we do it" then let me reinforce that I have no clue what you guys are up to. Except for the people in New Jersey. I have my suspicions about you folks and always have.

But that has more to do with them being from New Jersey than anything else.

Let's keep moving.

Basically, any local Masonic Lodge is a club. Masons call themselves a fraternity, but in my mind, I picture fraternities as being places with Greek names and naked college vixens hanging from the chandeliers. You will be highly disappointed if you join up thinking people are doing keg stands behind closed doors.

Until recently, none of the Masonic instruction was allowed to be written down. It had to be taught verbally from instructor to student over a period of months, and practiced relentlessly until the degree could be imparted without flaw. The trouble is that there is no other specific instruction on how to be a "Good Freemason" aside from that which is imparted during the degree.

Of course there are hundreds of books and websites that tell you to BE a good Freemason, but the parts that say, "A good freemason wakes up early on Sunday, mows his grass, eats a few fruits and grains and feeds stray dogs. On Monday he toils in the field, builds a tree house, and learns to play the kazoo," do not exist.

If the concern is that this group of mainly old men and curious young upstarts that meets once a month is somehow conspiring to control the World Bank, you are seriously deluded. The most controversial thing I've seen is a debate about who's going to cater the next meeting and what members will volunteer to wash the dishes during the pancake breakfast.

Inauspicious Beginnings

Real masons are referred to as Operative Masons. Those are the guys who point, grout, lay concrete and build foundations.

Speculative Masons, like me, are the guys who meet at the lodge and discuss the formation of building temples within each individual member.

Looking back, it's always been pretty clear which type of Mason I would wind up being. When I was fifteen years old, my dad hired a stonemason to build a new front deck on our house.

My dad, ever the spendthrift, graciously offered my services to this man free of charge. He did this, of course, without bothering to ask me or ever even tell me about it.

I got off of the school bus one sunny afternoon to see this very large, burly man covered in concrete dust standing by my front door. "Hey kid," he said. "Pick up that wheelbarrow and make me some mud."

I set down my schoolbag and said, "Excuse me?" All I had wanted to do that day was pour myself a nice glass of lemonade and read a few comic books. The prospect of getting filthy for no pay did not seem very appealing.

He grunted at me when he said, "Pick up that wheelbarrow right there, and go make me a batch of mud. I need it quick. Your dad said you were working with me, so get to it."

I looked up at him. "Mud?"

He looked at me like I was an idiot. I shrugged my shoulders and said, "Okay."

I wheeled the wheelbarrow into the backyard and found a shovel in the barn. I found a nice patch of soft grass and started to dig and dig until there were piles of dirt and grass inside the wheelbarrow's bucket. After it was full, I picked up the handles and drove the thing back into the front yard. The mason was up on a ladder, carefully setting a stone in place.

I grabbed a hose from the side of the house and started spraying it into the bucket, until there was so much water inside the wheelbarrow that clumps of dirt started to spill over the side. I grabbed one of the mason's hammers and began to stir.

At some point, this enormous man looked down at what I was doing from high up on the ladder. All I remember is looking back up at him and seeing his amazed, wide-eyed expression, to which I dutifully responded, "Your mud is almost ready, sir!"

And that was how my career as an Operative Mason began and ended. I picked up my schoolbag and went inside to set about doing what I'd wanted to do in the first place. It was not until my father came home that I was finally told that "mud" meant concrete to *some* people. Luckily, the mason was not interested in my returning to his worksite and opted to forge ahead without me.

History: Quick and Dirty

More than anything else, the Masonic connection to the Knights Templar has always fascinated me and drawn me to learning more about it. Freemasonry has an ancillary body that calls itself the Knights Templar, and even though they deny any historical ancestry, the evidence suggests otherwise.

The first thing we should do is get our historical understanding straight. Sit up, class. Get your pencils ready.

Since the dawn of time, people have sought to build things. They needed good, solid structures for government buildings, statues, temples, residences, and fortifications. It probably seemed like a good idea that if you were building a house, you'd want the people putting it together to have some idea about what they're doing. In those days before Better Business Bureaus, they needed a way to ensure that trained personnel were up to the task they were being paid for.

Kind of like the guy that shows up offering to repave your driveway.

It is up to you to decide if he is from a reputable asphalt company or a gypsy scam artist. I'm thinking that the station wagon with two buckets of Home Depot driveway sealer in the back are a pretty good indicator, but far be it from me to get involved with your business.

Anyway, the creation of a guild of Masons.

Given that the privilege of reading and writing was not available to much of the public, other ways were developed of ensuring that if a person said they were a member of the Mason's Guild, it could be proven. Secret words, handshakes, signs and many other forms of recognition were created to enable a Mason to travel around the country freely. They were a way of identifying yourself as a trained craftsman to others. A kind of primitive business card, if you will, but one that was only handed out to deserving recipients.

Severe punishments awaited those who somehow learned the secret ways of identifying themselves as Masons under false pretenses. These were unforgiving, hardened men who knew how to use the power tools of their times. Not people to be taken lightly, for sure.

One benefit of being an Operative Mason during this time was that Masons were one of the only classes of people allowed to travel freely from city to city. By virtue of the need to have them working at any given job site at any given time, the rulers of the kingdoms didn't want them tied up at the gatehouse.

This plays a very significant part in our story.

Over time, during the 16th or 17th Century, arose what we now call Speculative Freemasonry. It was a group of men who adopted the system created by their Operative brethren, but instead of physically building temples for kings, the idea was to erect a "temple" within each individual member.

There is no definitive answer as to why so many Freemasons abandoned the practical application of their trades and began focusing instead on character-development and solidarity. Historians can only guess as to how and why this occurred.

From what I've read, the answers can be found in the history of the Knights Templar.

After Jerusalem was captured during the First Crusade, many Christians wanted to make pilgrimages to the Holy Lands that so many had died to secure. Getting there was a harrowing task, and many of the pilgrims were robbed or killed while travelling there.

In the early 1100's a group of Knights were established to protect these travelling Christians and took on the name Knights Templar. The Catholic Church bestowed an official endorsement on them and the Templars began expanding rapidly. Many charities were directed toward the Order, and in 1139, the Pope declared that they were exempt from paying taxes.

And then, the Knights Templar had a moment of pure genius. They erected temples all along the path to Jerusalem, which were actually secret banking locations.

Travelers were able to deposit money at one temple and withdraw it at any other temple along the way. For a small fee.

This early foray into franchise banking worked well. Staggeringly well.

It worked too damn well.

The Knights Templar amassed SO much money that King Philip the IV of France had to borrow from them to finance his war with the English. The problem was, the Knights Templar actually expected to be paid back. There are, of course, certain risks associated with having a King owe you more money than he is interested in repaying.

In 1306 King Philip went to Pope Clement V and arranged to have the Templars outlawed and branded heretics. This left all of the Templars vast resources to be divvied up between the Church and State, because after all, why should a group of Satan worshippers be allowed to live, let alone have any money?

Pretty convenient, eh?

The Templar's Grand Master Jacques de Molay was arrested and tortured, until he gave a forced "confession" against the Order, and the witch hunt began. From May Tenth to May Twelfth, 1310, fifty four Templar Knights were burned at the stake.

On March Eighteenth, 1314, Jacques de Molay and another high-ranking Knight were the final imprisoned Templars to be executed via burning. According to legend, just prior to being burned, De Molay recanted his confession and declared the innocence of his brothers. He laid a curse upon the King and his all his descendants. He then ordered that both King Philip and Pope Clement V appear before God to answer for their crimes before the year was out.

Oddly enough, both the King and Pope were dead before the end of 1314. Stranger still, King Philip's House of Capet, which had ruled strong for 300 years, collapsed shortly thereafter.

Interestingly enough, the Freemasons youth chapter is called the Order of Demolay. Bill Clinton was a member, although he never pursued becoming a Freemason as an adult. This is often the source of confusion with Clinton being associated with the fraternity. Actually, he's a member of the Illuminati and a reptilian replacement from aliens seeking to overthrow the planet.

Oh, you think that's funny?

Just wait until we get into the discussion about conspiracy theories.

No one truly knows how many Templar Knights escaped persecution. What is certain is that they needed a way to escape the long-reaching arm of the church and state and flee as quickly and quietly as possible. In my opinion, there would have been no better way than by infiltrating and posing as Operative Masons.

By the mid-1700's, Speculative Freemasonry began incorporating the symbols and traditions of the Knights Templar. Whether this is by the design of self-aggrandizing members of the fraternity who wanted to pose as mystical descendants from a famous secret society, or it is by the merging of the two entities, none can say.

Mysteries abound about the history of Freemasonry as a whole, even from the members within it. However, the history of individual lodges, and the members that belonged to it, is expertly documented. My lodge has photographs of every Worshipful Master who has sat in the East since we were first chartered. Various ledgers of the Blue Lodge and the different bodies contain records, seals, and documentation about every individual member.

Someday, my descendants will be able to research my activity in the Lodge and see things written in my own hand. It is the chance to be a part of something that will remain.

For the record, I am also a Royal Arch Mason and a Knight Templar. I am a York Rite Mason, and have not considered the Scottish Rite as of yet. The Scottish Rite have a rarely given (or at least, more rarely given than all the other degrees) 33rd Degree that is supposed to be reserved for special members.

Of course, this has led to an entire new branch of conspiracy theorists who claim that while the rest of Freemasonry might just be a bunch of old guys sitting around wearing aprons, its these sinister 33rd Degrees who are really up to no good.

I have no idea, but if I were to eventually pursue the Scottish Rite with the goal in mind of reaching the 33rd

Degree then…then you will all quake in fear at the mention of my very name and bow to my iron will (cue evil laugh).

But in all likelihood, it's just more spaghetti dinners to organize.

Sigh. This ruling the world by being a part of an all-powerful multi-national conspiracy that secretly controls the planet is a bummer sometimes.

Chapter 2: Proof of a Conspiracy! Or, Something Close to It

    Let's talk money, baby. Dollars and cents. Euros. Paper bills etched with secret codes and meanings familiar only to the Masonic eye that only a few bold outsiders were wise enough to unravel. Because really, what's the motivation for being in a secret organization that rules the planet if you can't control all the cash?

    We'll start with the American dollar bill.

The All-Seeing Eye

The pyramid with an eye positioned on top of it is one of the most familiar symbols of Freemasonry as it is associated with its pervasive influence over the United States. "Ah ha!" they say. "There it is, evidence of a conspiracy."

Except it actually isn't.

Americans can find the eye on top of the pyramid on our one-dollar bills as well as the reverse side of the United States Seal, but it appears in various other mediums, including Renaissance art and Egyptian mythology. It gets labeled as everything from the "Eye of God" to the "Evil Eye."

The reverse side of the United States Seal bears the words *Annuit Cœptis* on either side of the eye, which translates as: "He approves our undertakings." The script along the bottom of the pyramid reading *Novus Ordo Seclorum* means: "New Order of the Ages."

Incidentally, as I'm sure you're wondering, "New Order of the Ages" is not a cute way of saying "New World Order." It's a quote from Virgil's poem "Eclogue IV."

The pyramid is composed of thirteen steps, which represent the thirteen original states, with the base level bearing Roman Numerals for 1776.

It is, for all intents and purposes, an artistic interpretation of the then-fledgling nation to grow and prosper with the hope that God was looking down over them.

Until you see the upside down pentagram it *clearly* is meant to depict.

The Upside Down Goathead Pentagram of EVIL

Follow me on this one. If you take the first letter of "Anno" and the last letter of "Coeptis" as it appears on the US Seal, then connect the first letter of "Novus," the last letter of "Ordo," and the last letter of "Seclorum," and you've got an upside down pentagram.

Even more sinister, those letters spell out the word M-A-S-O-N.

Well…not exactly. If you go left to right, they actually spell A-S-N-O-M. They also spell out: AMSON, MANSO, SAMON, NOMSA, etc.

But still this damning evidence is irrefutable by everyone on the planet, excepting those with more than a half-dozen synapses firing in their brain at any given time.

Eagles and Owls on Our Dollars, Oh My!

Talk about jumping on the bandwagon. The Grand Lodge of Texas Freemasons published an article in 1955 that claimed the eagle on the dollar bill had clear significance to Masonic Lore. They said that since the Eagle's wings had thirty-two feathers on one side, thirty-three on the other side and nine tail feathers, it was clear that they meant the 32 Degrees of Scottish Rite Freemasonry, the ever secretive 33rd Degree of Scottish Rite, and 9 Degrees for all of the ones found in the York Rite.

We're going to get into the various degrees later on, but follow me on this one. The nine degrees in York Rite Masonry are completely different and exist within absolutely separate bodies. Nothing like the lazy Scottish Rite Masons who go for a weekend and come back with thirty-two Degrees in their cap.

Yes, I'm taking a playful shot at my Scottish Rite Masonic brothers, because in York Rite you actually have to participate in all of the degrees your receive, one at a time.

Sissies.

Just kidding.

Doesn't make it any less true though.

But anyway, thanks a bunch 1955 Texas Grand Lodge for heaping more speculative logs on the fire. They even went further to say that all the feathers put together totaled sixty-five, which is CLEARLY meant to signify a Hebrew phrase ("Yam Yawchod") which is CLEARLY a reference to the First Degree.

I think I'd like to speak for everyone present when I say: Seriously, guys, WTF?

The owl that can only be seen if you know to look for it appears in the upper right hand corner of the 1's that appear surrounding George Washington on the dollar bill.

Does the owl have any special significance to Freemasonry?

Nope.

But apparently the owl's status as an object of the occult (You know, Merlin had an owl, Harry Potter had an owl…we're talking about witchcraft folks. Evil, dark, sinister witchcraft. Hide your kids, hide your wife, etc etc) it somehow gets lumped in as further evidence of the Mason's involvement with the secret underpinnings of the American government.

In actuality, the all-seeing eye was designed by a non-mason named Pierre Du Simitiere. The only actual Freemason on the original committee that designed the United States seal was Benjamin Franklin. Franklin's proposal did not have an eye on it, and the others rejected it.

If you examine things at face value, the essential logic goes like this:

There are secret Masonic symbols etched into the dollar bill for the United States of America.

Therefor the Masons secretly run the World Bank.

The World Bank is obviously controlled by the people looking to instill a New World Order.

The Masons are going to kill everyone on the planet.

I can't even freaking make sense of it and I'm sitting here looking at all of their mixed up gibberish claiming to be evidence of the whole thing. It's just silly.

Unlike the damn Europeans. We Americans are just misunderstood but those bastards across the pond are REALLY up to no good.

In 2002 twelve European countries agreed to operate under one unified currency called the Euro.

(Cue Organ Chords) Duh Duh Duhhhhhhhh.

And because now the European countries involved (called the Eurozone. Sounds like a fun place to me. Some kind of club where all the guys are in black turtlenecks smoking long, thin cigarettes and the women are sexy, exotic types.) are moving toward the elimination of hard currency to replace it with devious things like debit cards.

And we know how that one goes.

No more hard currency?

Chips in the brains of our children by the government and Antichrist taking over.

Bam. One, two, three, you're pinned, Free World.

Good thing *SOME* people were paying attention.

All right, show of hands. How many of you stopped reading this chapter to go look at a dollar bill in your wallet?

Know how I knew that?

Evil Masonic Kindle Book Telepathic Mind Control Conspiracy, suckers. Take that.

Chapter 3: An Incomplete but Still Thoroughly Engaging List of People Who Were Freemasons

Given that Freemasonry has existed for such a long period of time, it stands to reason that there have been a large multitude of members that have travelled through its ranks. While it is not the worldwide historical conspiracy that some people insist, it is still mind-boggling at the sheer number of influential people who belonged to the fraternity.

This is not a complete list of notable masons, just the ones I thought notable or interesting enough to write down.

Plenty of very important historical people were also Freemasons who I have left out, but I still included Bronson Pinchot. Why? Because I found out he was and said, "Seriously? Balki?"

Historical figures:

Benedict Arnold, Simon Bolivar, Daniel Boone, James Bowie, Winston Churchill, William "Buffalo Bill" Cody, Samuel Colt, Charles "The Count of Auschwitz" Coward, Davy Crockett, Benjamin Franklin, John Glenn, John Hancock, Patrick Henry, J. Edgar Hoover, Sam Houston, Andrew Jackson, Marquis de Lafayette, Dr. Charles Mayo, Wolfgang Amadeus Mozart, Paul Revere, Franklin D. Roosevelt, Harry Truman, George Washington

It's really no surprise that so many influential members of the American Revolution were also Freemasons. The birth of the United States is steeped in Masonic tradition, all of which has been well-documented both for historical purposes and crude sensationalism. There are large numbers of important figures from both the Revolutionary War and the Civil War that I did not include, but are still worth researching.

Modern Era Politicians:

Gerald Ford, Robert Dole, Rev. Jesse Jackson

I can't really say why Gerald Ford and Bob Dole don't impress me but Jesse Jackson does. I think it's because it's just a bizarre person to associate with Freemasonry. I mean, Ford and Dole are both crusty old white guys, and I'm pretty sure every single crusty old white guy in politics is suspected of being one as well. But Jesse Jackson? Didn't see that one coming.

Sports Figures:

Ty Cobb, Jack Dempsey, Rogers Hornsby, Shaquille O'Neal, Sugar Ray Robinson, Cy Young

Okay, now take a quick look at that group and tell me which one you didn't expect to see. Chances are, if you're my age, you first became familiar with Shaq as one of the two-man team on NBA Jams in the arcades as a kid. "He's heating up!" Indeed. On another note, I'm always kind of embarrassed to see Ty Cobb's name in there. Talk about not exhibiting Masonic principals. Cobb was a racist, a poor sportsman, a woman beater, and an all-around A-hole.

Business Moguls:

Bob Evans, Henry Ford, Richard Gatling, John Gates, Frederick Maytag, The Ringling Brothers, Col. Harland Sanders, Dave Thomas, John Wanamaker

Some interesting names in there, but none more so than the Ringling Brothers. All seven of them. I'm pretty sure that's enough people to start your own lodge. Although, you have to admit, spaghetti dinners would be pretty interesting if you had all of the Ringling Brothers hosting. I'd be expecting jugglers and fire-eaters to come popping out of the kitchen every time.

Actors and Entertainers:

Gene Autry, Johann Christian Bach, Mel Blanc, Ernest Borgnine, Samuel Clemons, Nat 'King' Cole, Sir Arthur Conan Doyle, Duke Ellington, Douglas Fairbanks, Clark Gable, Oliver Hardy, Harry Houdini, Rudyard Kipling, Audie Murphy, Bronson Pinchot, Richard Pryor, Michael Richards, Roy Rogers, Will Rogers, Telly Savalas, Peter Sellers, Red Skelton, John Wayne, Oscar Wilde

I wonder if all those old timey Western actors were Masons before they went to Hollywood? If that's the case, then I think we might have just uncovered an actual Masonic conspiracy. These are a group of men who infiltrated the movie industry and conspired to wear tall hats and pants with tassels. Impressive. But there it is: Bronson Pinchot. I'd make fun of Bronson Pinchot, but hey, at least he had the dignity to never perform at the Laugh Factory and go on a racist tirade. Isn't that right, Michael Richards? Interestingly enough, after Richards embarrassed himself he turned to notable black leaders to apologize and seek guidance. Who was number one on his list? None other than fellow Mason, Jesse Jackson!

Chapter 4: The Internet, or, Affirmations for Silly People

Listen, I know this will come as a surprise to most of you, so I'm going to try and break the news as gently as possible.

People are stupid.

And nowhere on the entire planet Earth are people more willing to demonstrate exactly how stupid they are than on the internet. Sadly enough, great heaping hordes of other stupid people are willing to devour the drivel that appears online and take it as gospel.

If you go on any number of websites, you will see the following people held up to be Freemasons or members of some other nefarious, world-dominating group. The justifications for these insinuations is so convoluted that you'd have to be a complete jello-head to give them any credence, and yet…well, there must be a good amount of jello-heads out there.

Some are pretty obvious as to why people like to claim they are Freemasons, such as:

Tony Blair, George H.W. Bush, George W. Bush, Dick Cheney, Bill Clinton, L. Ron Hubbard, Barack Obama, Colin Powell, and Ronald Reagan

Nearly any controversial or powerful modern political figure is associated with the Fraternity, normally as a way of justifying their popularity. Normally, the people asserting that so-and-so must be Freemason is on the other side of the political fight from the person their accusing.

It's basically a way of saying, "This complete moron could not possibly have risen to power unless they had the support of Illuminati behind him. I mean, the guy is hardly smart enough to tie his own shoes."

Some of the more amusing allegations of Freemasonry are leveled against modern celebrities, with my all-time favorites being

Sean (Jay-Z) Carter and Kanye West

The reasons for this are so completely crazy that it would take a whole book to psychoanalyze the paranoid, misinformed goofiness that goes into them. Essentially, it can be boiled down to a few things. Both men are rich, successful, and powerful in their respective fields.

I've seen countless articles that claim to have proof of their connection to either Freemasonry or the Illuminati based on their jewelry, t-shirt designs, hand gestures and lyrics to their songs.

It is like claiming certain rock groups are encouraging people to worship Satan by spinning their albums backwards. Complete silliness.

Unless we are talking about Simon and Garfunkel. For some reason, when I hear their music, I want to run screaming through the city streets. They either have hidden messages in their music or I just really can't stand them.

Incidentally, do you remember the scene in Fight Club when Tyler Durdin asks who you would fight out of anyone in the world if you had a chance? Mine would be Simon and Garfunkel. I have the battle plan worked out in my head, where I go for Paul Simon first because he's smaller and looks sneakier.

You're still with me on this one, right? I can't be the only person having these thoughts.

And finally, the two funniest names of people I found who are "accused" of being Freemasons on the internet are:

Leonardo da Vinci and Williams Shakespeare

I'm not even sure what to really say to that. Poor Leo sure does get dragged through the mud a lot these days. Whether people are claiming he painted himself as a woman in the Mona Lisa or he somehow stole all of his ideas from aliens who abducted him, it's somehow fashionable to discredit the man.

As for Billy the Bard, your guess is as good as mine. I would think that in between rewriting the King James Bible and stealing all of those works of literature from Christopher Marlowe or his wife Anne Hathaway, he'd have been too busy to be a Freemason.

And just for the record, that's the Anne Hathaway he married, not the actress.

Although, I'm sure if we really put our minds together, we can cook up a whole new conspiracy theory that brings all of these wonderful elements into play. Perhaps during his alien abduction/time travel escapades, Leonard da Vinci picked up William Shakespeare and whisked him all the way to modern times where he found nubile Anne Hathaway slaving over a series of unproduced movie scripts. He stole the plots from the movies, and da Vinci stole the space age technology that appeared in them. Each of them went back to their separate times and carried on like they'd created something special. And then Jay-Z used the powers of Baphomet to trick Beyonce into marrying him. Bam!

Admittedly, it's kind of farfetched, but if we couldn't get at least a dozen people to believe it just because it's written on the internet, I'll eat my hat.

Chapter 5: Which Brings Us to Jack the Ripper

Anyone who tells you they know who Jack the Ripper really was is wildly arrogant and sadly uninformed.

Here's the truth, folks: Nobody knows and nobody ever will.

I spent an entire year researching the Jack the Ripper crimes for my book WHITECHAPEL: THE FINAL STAND OF SHERLOCK HOLMES. I built timelines, studied autopsy reports, worked with the FBI Behavioral Sciences Unit, and read newspaper accounts until my eyes started to go numb.

One of the worst mistakes any criminal investigator can make is developing a theory first, then structuring their investigation to support that theory.

Imagine if one of your neighbors was found murdered, and the detective who showed up took one look at the crime scene and said, "I bet that guy who lives next door did it."

The detective then based every single investigative decision around proving it was you who killed the person. At the end of the day, you'd be arrested, and the case would be based on a series of shaky assumptions.

That is exactly what happens with Jack the Ripper nowadays. Not just with the Freemasons, either. Any random name that pops up from history is given the once-over by amateur Ripperologists who doggedly seek to pin the crimes on him.

And for the record, amateur Ripperologists aren't just pimply youths in their mother's basements logging onto Casebook.org. In 2002, best-selling novelists Patricia Cornwell got it into her head that world famous painter Walter Sickert must have been the culprit.

She published a book titled PORTRAIT OF A KILLER: JACK THE RIPPER – CASE CLOSED in which she systematically accused Sickert of all those horrible crimes. What was her evidence, you ask?

Well…mainly, he painted things that appeared to be scary and unkind to women.

Wait, you mean that's not enough to convince you?

She conducted DNA testing on stamps licked by the painter and had handwriting analysis done on the alleged Ripper letters and destroyed a valuable painting all in the effort to prove her initial thought. And what did it gain her?

People like me laughing at her.

Jack the Ripper, case closed. Indeed.

The list of Ripper suspects is endlessly amusing, and it includes people like Lewis Carrol (author of Alice in Wonderland), Prince Albert, and Jill the Ripper. Among the top of the list, however, are the more serious suspects and who among us has not heard of poor Sir William Gull?

Gull is the perfect Jack the Ripper suspect. Made to order. You couldn't ask for juicier subject matter. First, Gull was the royal physician to Queen Victoria. Second, he was a Freemason.

Guilty.

Reams and reams of volumes of books, films, articles, and internet sites have been devoted to proving William Gull was Jack the Ripper. By association, this also drags in the Royal Family and the entire Masonic Order into the equation. Pretty good bargain for conspiracy theorists, I must say.

Except for one tiny detail. In 1887 Gull began to experience a series of strokes brought on by a cerebral hemorrhage. These events left him partially paralyzed and the strokes continued until he passed away in 1890. He was seventy-three years old.

Pishaw! Why let the facts get in the way of a good story? People find all sorts of ways to get around that information, and often tie it into the crimes themselves. They say that William Gull committed the Jack the Ripper crimes precisely because he was sick. As if some kind of brain fever spurred Gull on to unleash his fury upon the whores of Whitechapel.

I'd ask them to find me one example in human history of a septuagenarian who went on a killing spree after suffering a debilitating stroke and partial paralysis. If that's the case, I think we need to start keeping a closer eye on these old fogies before they kill again.

The real culprit in all of this silliness is a man named Stephen Knight.

Knight was a British…*author*…(pains me to say it)…who wrote a book called Jack the Ripper: The Final Solution in 1976. He interviewed a man named Joseph Gorman (who was claiming to be named Joseph Sickert. Yes, the illegitimate son of that same Walter Sickert that Patricia Cornwell went after.) who laid out a wild story of murder, conspiracy and Masonic involvement to cover up the bad deeds of the Royal Family.

This book went through twenty editions and is still a cornerstone of Ripperologist and conspiracy theorist thought.

And it was all a hoax. Gorman told The Sunday Times of London "It was a hoax; I made it all up...a whopping fib."

Of course, that didn't stop old Stephen Knight from keeping the book going, and it didn't stop people from gobbling up the lies and regurgitating them as if they were fact. This practice continues to this day, and frankly, it sickens me.

There are multiple "links" between the manner in which the Ripper victims were dispatched and displayed as well as geographical links to the locations of the crimes and Masonic tradition. For example, Catherine Eddowes, the fourth Ripper victim, was killed at Mitre Square.

Both the mitre and square are stonemason's tools, and appear in Masonic traditions along with multiple others. But, according to Stephen Knight, this is the smoking gun that positively cements Masonic involvement in the Ripper crimes.

The Mitre and Square are traditional symbols of Freemasonry.

The fourth Ripper victim was killed at Mitre Square.

Eureka!

It sounds silly to me even as I write it, and yet, there are people who swear by this line of thought.

Masonic Method of Death

Often, the method in which the victims of Jack the Ripper were killed and displayed is linked to Freemasonry. Here is the evidence:

All of the victims had their throats cut.

Annie Chapman's intestines were displayed over her right shoulder.

Graffiti in a stairwell near Elizabeth Stride's body read "The Juwes Are the men that will not be blamed for nothing." Juwes is a Masonic reference.

Police Commissioner Sir Charles Warren immediately ordered the graffiti removed.

And finally, the most damning evidence of all:

The murder victims were all found in an upside down pentagram shape. There is also the same upside down pentagram shape formed by streets in Washington DC. See? You see? It's all coming together now, isn't it. You're nodding your head. You are starting to see through the lies and deceit of the Freemasons with their secret devil goat worship and Ripper killing Royal Family cover-ups.

I'm No Sherlock Holmes…

But I'm about as close as you're going to get when it comes to this subject matter. I'm not only an experienced criminal investigator, but I've studied the Ripper crimes extensively for my first book. I know what I'm talking about when it comes to this.

So here's the facts:

Yes, all of the Ripper victims had their throats cut. It was the most convenient way for the killer to dispatch his targets and keep them from screaming. London's East End was a busy district all times of day and night, and the killer needed time to perform his delusional rituals.

Annie Chapman's organs were displayed in a specific manner, but so were the rest of the victims in an increasingly elaborate fashion. All of that is consistent with a serial killer personality who is evolving in his dementia. The true reasons why Jack the Ripper chose to display his victims in that particular manner were known only to him. The same way that only Green River and BTK and Jeffrey Dahmer only know the real reasons they wanted to do what they did.

Graffiti on the stairwell was found near the second of two victims to fall in a single night. On September 30th 1888, Elizabeth Stride and Catherine Eddowes were both killed. Stride's throat was cut, but the killer was believed to be interrupted by a man named Louis Diemschutz as he returned home from work.

Approximately forty-five minutes later, Catherine Eddowes body was found in nearby Mitre Square. The fact that she was mutilated and murdered in a dark, unoccupied construction area, perfect for such business, is overlooked simply to point out the place was named MITRE SQUARE.

During the search for the killer, a police officer found a bloodstained apron in a stairwell on Goulston Street inside a tenement building. The bloodstained apron turned out to be a highly significant piece of evidence because it was directly matched to the one Eddowes was wearing when she was killed.

In all likelihood, the killer was fleeing the area as police flooded in and he ditched the apron in the stairwell in his attempt to get away and divest himself of evidence linking him to the crime.

So, why then wouldn't he take the time to write a little message?

Above the dirty apron on the wall (In the stairwell. In the tenement building. Yes, Virginia, they had graffiti in tenement buildings back then too.) was the infamous message: "The Juwes Are the men that will not be blamed for nothing."

And here's the kicker. Nobody in Freemasonry knows what the heck a "Juwe" is. It isn't part of any ritual. Never has been. Never will be.

The Police Commissioner at the time ordered the evidence destroyed because he was likely worried about people associating "Juwes" with the Jewish immigrants living nearby and causing a race war.

Here's the last word on Jack the Ripper. The Final Analysis. Something final and definitive since hoaxers love to punctuate their foolish opinions with some sort of title that leaves no room for doubt.

Jack the Ripper: The Go Away and Stop Bothering Me with Your Silly Theories Analysis

The only chance anyone ever had to catch Jack the Ripper came and went over one hundred years ago. Essential evidence was not obtained. The end. Everybody else is looking to get on television.

Chapter 6: Somewhere, a Whole Lot of Villages Are Missing Their Idiots

To try and describe and debunk all of the cockamamie paranoid delusions about Freemasonry would take more time and patience than I possess. Basically, if you're inclined to believe silliness, who am I to stop you?

That won't prevent me from listing some of the more bizarre anti-Masonic beliefs out there. Who knows, I might even be inclined to poke a little fun at you.

What, Me Catholic?

I've got bad news for you Catholics who would consider exploring Freemasonry. It will condemn you to Hell. Forever.

In 1983 the Pope himself forced a "Declaration on Masonic Associations" that not only condemned Freemasonry, but said any Catholics who join it are in grave sin and cannot partake in Holy Communion.

It is also asserted that "Masonic writings" deny God has revealed himself or ever established a church.

Now, as I've already told you, very little about Freemasonry is written down. If by "Masonic writings" they are referring to *any* writing done about Freemasonry or by a Freemason, then God knows what else Freemasonry stands for.

Pretty interesting that a fraternity with no central leadership linking all of the assorted Grand Lodges and no written doctrine managed to all come to such an important agreement.

The Judeo-Masonic Conspiracy

This one is simply astounding, not so much for the content of what it says, but for the reach that it had.

In 1903, a document titled The Protocols of the Elders of Zion was published in Russia. This pamphlet described a Jewish plot to take over the world and explained how they had infiltrated Freemasonry to accomplish this task. The Protocols quickly went viral, reaching multiple countries in multiple languages, spreading across the globe like pictures of Lindsey Lohan's nether regions.

Henry Ford had 500,000 copies printed and distributed throughout the United States, and Adolf Hitler ordered it taught to school children in Nazi classrooms. Most amazingly, it had already been debunked as a fraud.

The authors (eeek…okay, here I go having to use that term again) of the Protocols essentially stole large portions from a fictional work by Maurice Joly called Dialogue in Hell Between Machiavelli and Montesquieu.

As early as 1921 The Times of London was exposing the document as a forgery and a fraud, but people promptly ignored the facts and kept right on printing it.

Staggeringly, The Protocols of the Elders of Zion is credited with helping to form Adolph Hitler's thoughts on Jews and his eventual decision to engage in genocide.

New World Order

Essentially, NWO theorists believe that a secret group of powerful people are conspiring to rule the world through one government.

They believe, in no particular order as follows: The Antichrist will be in charge, as written in the Book of Revelations; the Freemasons and/or the Illuminati are secretly working to bring this all about; the NWO is the manifestation of the original plot first revealed in The Protocols of the Elders of Zion; it's all the work of aliens who are secretly replacing government officials with Reptile People.

Now, as bizarre as that sounds, it's all bonafide doctrine from New World Order theorists. My personal favorite is the Reptile People one. They're also called Reptilians, Reptoids, Reptiloids, and Draconians.

There is no way in the world you could possibly convince me that this is anything more than the fevered dream of overexcited paranoid schizophrenics…unless you stuck me in a room with Rick Santorum and Nancy Pelosi. Fifteen minutes in and I'd probably be right there with you.

Part of the problem is that people have blurred the lines between fiction and reality, and with the internet, speculation is often presented as fact. And, well…like I said, there's a lot of dummies out there who jump at the first thing they read.

Any cursory glance at "Freemason Conspiracy" on Google will reveal a wide array of statements made about "Masonic facts." Worshipping Satan is one that seems to pop up quite a bit.

As we previously discussed, the Knights Templar were declared to be heretics as early as the 1300's, because it was a simple way to discredit them, outlaw them, and steal their money.

Not much has changed.

Any rational person would look at the long, sordid history of misinformation and outright lies that surround all of these conspiracy theories and realize that it's a house of cards. Of course, the contributing factor to that outcome is "rational" people.

Chapter 7: But Wait, It Gets Better

Those devilish Freemasons. It isn't bad enough they scribbled graffiti all over our currency and Seal and hid their messages in our most important documents. They even went so far as to build the city of Washington DC in occult patterns.

There is an upside down pentagram formed by intersecting streets in DC. At the bottom of this unholy symbol is the White House.

Did all the blood just drain out of your face? Did you feel the chill running up and down your spine?

You should have, because from the bottom of this Satanic symbol is a SECOND Masonic malarkey. The Square and Compass go from the White House to the Capital Building, and then back down to the Jefferson Memorial.

Cue Organ Music: Duh duh duh duhhhhh.

Case closed. Freemasons in the White House. Antichrist taking over. New World Order. That's it.

…Except for one teeny tiny detail.

The streets don't actually *form* a pentagram. The actual streets that are said to form the pentagram (Rhode Island Ave., Vermont Ave., Massachusetts Ave., Connecticut Ave., and K Street) do not all connect. The maps used by conspirators to terrify the simple-minded overlook the way the streets of the city are actually shaped.

And even if there IS a pentagram on the streets (which there isn't), it would not make it necessarily evil or even

Masonic. According to an article by National Geographic in 2009, "The pentagram, for example, is much older than Freemasonry and acquired its occult overtones only in the 19th and 20th centuries, hundreds of years after the Masons had adopted the symbol."

There are four obelisks in major Western cities across the world. London, Paris, New York City, and Washington DC. And all of them are evil. Just ask your local nutcase.

Here goes the logic:

Obelisks originated in ancient Egypt.

They were dedicated to Osiris, an Egyptian deity.

"Some" Masons think (I love that caveat. There's a Masonic lodge in how many thousands of cities and counties and villages all across the world, all filled with Masons, and SOME of them believe in one particular thing. Perfect!) that Osiris was later reborn as Hiram Abiff.

Hiram Abiff is a very important figure in Masonic lore.

Therefor all of these obelisks are indicative of the world's pending enslavement to the Freemasons.

I notice that I keep petering out at the final reveal for those. There's this big build up and I kind of softball it at the end. I can't help it really. By the time I've gotten that far, I just can't bring myself to tie it all together as nicely as the wackadoos do.

Listen, I'm sure if you go on any of the many websites claiming to tell you the real truth about Freemasonry you'll get a better idea of how all this stuff means the world is ending and the reptilian people are taking over.

My brain starts to hurt when I try to think like them. It truly does.

Chapter 8: Blame It On Albert Pike (I Do)

Most of the ammunition the nutballs use against Freemasonry can be traced back to one man: Albert Pike. Pike was born in 1809, and throughout the remainder of his life, he certainly got around. A quick glance at his curriculum vitae reveals that Pike was:

An attorney, a Brigadier-General in the Confederate Army, a 33rd Degree Mason in the Scottish Rite, and a member of the Knights of the Ku Klux Klan.

Pretty dodgy stuff, indeed. But there is apparently more to know about Albert Pike, depending on who you ask. Pike is often accused of being a Satanist, and also for establishing the blueprint for the New World Order.

Because being a racist Satanist Confederate General high-ranking official in the KKK just isn't enough, this guy just had to be an attorney too?

Shudder.

Pike is the only Confederate officer who has a statue in Washington DC, and people routinely point to his connection to Freemasonry as the reason it is allowed to exist.

Interestingly enough, he did not have much of a military career.

Pike was a veteran of the Mexican-American war, but never held a position higher than Troop Commander. Later, when the Civil War broke out, Pike was appointed as a military envoy to the Native Americans, and his successful negotiation of several treaties led to him being awarded a high-ranking position in the Confederate Army.

He led an Indian cavalry in the Battle of Pea Ridge, in which he was defeated. After the Battle, he was accused of theft and atrocities and fled. Pike was later arrested and charged with treason and insubordination, but upon his resignation from the Confederate Army, he was released.

And this is the guy they gave the one single Confederate Army statue to?

While much about Albert Pike is in dispute, including his affiliation with the KKK or what office he held, everyone is sure of one thing.

He was an…(grrrrrr)…author.

Pike wrote the book MORALS AND DOGMA OF THE ANCIENT AND ACCEPTED SCOTTISH RITE OF

FREEMASONRY. This book was presented to all new Scottish Rite initiates from the early 1900's to the late 1960's.

The book itself describes the various degrees of the Scottish Rite in a series of essays. It's full of parables, and not nearly as inflammatory as the other things Pike wrote, such as editorials and letters spelling out his racist beliefs.

Personally, I'm not fan of Albert Pike.

I wish they'd take his damn statue down, not only to rip a fang out of the conspiracy theory people's maws, but because it is simply undeserved. The guy was a bum.

Of course, taking down the statue won't satisfy the fruitcakes, now will it? They're too busy sniffing out Pike's alleged connections to the Illuminati.

The story goes like this: Albert Pike was a friend of an Italian revolutionary named Giusseppe Mazzini. Mazzini was a 33rd Degree Scottish Rite Mason who took over the Illuminati in 1834 and then founded the mafia.

Pike reportedly wrote a letter to Mazzini that spelled out his entire plan for the Illuminati to institute a New World Order. They were going to instigate three world wars and two revolutions.

After Mazzini died, Albert Pike instilled a new leader of the Illuminati and then proceeded to set up new Supreme Councils around the world.

Sounds pretty good right? Hot stuff indeed.

It's all made up.

There is no proof that any letter was ever written between Albert Pike and Giusseppe Mazzini. For as much as the whackos like to say "The letter was once displayed at the British Museum," they just can't seem to find the date or any actual reference to the letter by the Museum itself. The Museum has come out and said that they never displayed the letter.

Even though the letter has never been seen, read, or reproduced, nutjobs still somehow manage to have quotes from it. And not just any quotes. The ones that illustrate the plans for each sinister World War and how the Zionists and Islamists and Illuminati and blah blah blah blah are all going to come together to finally instill a NEW WORLD ORDER.

If I never read the words *Zionist, New World Order, Illuminati,* or *pentagram* again, it will be too soon.

Anyway, that's Albert Pike.

Chapter 9: And With All That Said, Something IS Rotten in Denmark

I think one of the reasons the prejudices against Freemasonry exist is that people do suspect that something is fundamentally wrong with the systems that control our lives.

Me too.

I just don't happen to think it's got anything to do with the group of old guys in my Masonic Lodge who can't organize more than a spaghetti dinner once a month. I also don't think it's got to do with Illuminati, alien invasions, Reptilians, or Zionists.

I think those are the fantastical dreams of simplistic minds, the kind that can conceive of a problem, but have no ability to grasp its actual cause. Kind of like physicians in ancient times who realized people were getting sick and decided that cutting them open to get rid of the "bad blood" was the perfect solution.

Primitive cultures who looked at an active volcano and said, "If that volcano goes up, we're all going to be wiped out. It must be an angry volcano god. I know, we'll chuck a virgin into it to make him happy."

Confronting a simpleton can be a tricky proposition. Especially when you present them with undeniable facts that challenge something they believe whole-heartedly.

Many years ago, I was working with an older gentleman who promptly informed me that George

Washington was not the first President of the United States of America.

"Say again?" I said.

"George Washington wasn't the first President. There was a whole bunch of Presidents before him, but it's kept a secret. We had Black Presidents, Native American Presidents, all that, but the government has conspired to keep this fact from us."

I was both amused and confused by this information. For one, it seemed too bizarre to pay any attention to, but at the same time, he was so serious about it that I thought it worth looking into. I did a little research and the next time I saw my friend, I told him what I'd found.

"George Washington was the first President of the United States. Period. Prior to him, and before the United States government was formed, there was something called the President of the Continental Congress. There were sixteen of these Presidents, and they had almost no executive powers."

He just stared at me.

"Also, they were all crusty old white guys."

His eyes narrowed on me, they took on a decidedly unfriendly glaze.

I dug deep for something, thinking on my feet, trying to keep him on my side. "I bet they were all *Freemasons*," I whispered knowingly.

This grown man looked me up and down and said, "I already knew about *those* Presidents, but they weren't the ones I was talking about." With that, he turned his back on my and walked away. We never discussed the matter again.

Too much knowledge with too little information about the subject is a dangerous combination. Unfortunately, everywhere you look today there are so-called experts dialoging freely about subjects with which they have very little facts. Worse still, there are others who read that garbage and accept it verbatim and then go around spewing it to others.

So like I said, I do believe that the systems that control the United States and the world at large are flawed, corrupt, and always seeking to strengthen their grip on the working man. I just don't think it's anything as romantic as some shadowy secret society. I bet it's just some corporate policy for a conglomerate of oil companies, or lobbyists trying to drain funds from the American people for their own personal gain.

And that's the real danger in people who waste their time believing in conspiracies. They are too busy about worrying if Barack Obama is an American citizen (He is.

Enough already) or if George Bush was a Freemason (He wasn't) to see what is being stolen right out from under them.

There are some very real dangers out there from gigantic, international organizations who threaten our individual existences and they don't plot to make Jay-Z the head of Def Jam or help the Jews maintain control of Israel. They are Corporate Agriculture who fill up our supermarkets with genetically modified animals and grains. They are Big Oil manipulating the prices and debilitating alternative research. Very real, very dangerous, and very serious about getting what they want.

But when they took over, I guess we were all too worried about the Reptilians.

Chapter 10: Questions about Freemasonry

I'd like to qualify my answers by saying that I am not an expert. I have done a fair bit of reading and research, and have tried to give the most informed answers here, but I reserve the right to be dead-wrong. If that happens, I assure you that it is a mistake made of sheer misunderstanding, and that it was unintentional.

Also, I don't pretend to speak for anyone other than myself. This is my personal perspective on Freemasonry, as it pertains to me.

Is Freemasonry only for men? Do they admit women? If not, why not?

In America, only men can be Freemasons. I've heard that they have a couple female Freemasons floating around Europe, but I would imagine it is not the norm.

There are several masonic organizations for women. The Eastern Star has a group that meets at my lodge. I don't know much about them, other than that they do degree work for their members, have rituals, and really kick ass in terms of fundraising.

Is it a Secret Society or just a Society with Secrets?

I would say that Freemasonry is very-much a society with secrets, in that members don't hide their affiliation or meeting places. Freemasons are a properly registered body. That being said, there are many things that are only shared with the members and not with outsiders.

What do you DO at these meetings?

It depends on the type of meeting. A general ("stated") meeting occurs monthly, where the body of Master Masons discuss lodge affairs and vote on new members. Sometimes a guest lecturer is invited to discuss a wide variety of topics.

Extra meetings are held for new members to receive requisite degrees that will make them into full members. There are three degrees in Freemasonry: 1st Degree (Entered Apprentice), 2nd Degree (Fellowcraft) and 3rd (Master Mason). The associated bodies have additional degrees that are considered off-shoots and do not put any member of those organizations, no matter how high-ranking, above members of the Blue Lodge.

What is the stated purpose of the society?

Hmm. Tough one. As I've already said, there is no singular unifying body in Freemasonry. Every state is governed by its Grand Lodge and they take a varied approach to the practice of Freemasonry. Thus, what you read on the internet about how things are done in Utah will be very, very different from how it is done in Pennsylvania.

Freemasonry is one of the largest charitable organizations in the world, but it is not a charity. All Shriners are Masons (But not vice-versa), therefore you can count every Shriner Hospital as a part of the Masons charitable efforts. Thousands and thousands of children all around the world have received free state-of-the-art health care at Shriner Hospitals.

A large portion of Freemasonry is dedicated to self-preservation. Very little is written down in The Craft, and older members must constantly educate younger ones, ensuring that the ritual and meaning is passed down properly. Freemasonry only exists because generations of men have made sure it stayed strong and healthy.

How do new members get in?

Ask a Mason to join. No one is ever supposed to be recruited into Freemasonry. You are supposed to go to a member of the Lodge and ask to join. (Don't let that idea intimidate you. In this modern era, most Lodges have a website. If you don't know any actual Masons, just email the secretary of the Lodge and ask if they can help you out.

Someone will be glad to help you out. There are special recognitions for those who bring new members into the Lodge.)

I say "supposed" in the above paragraph because I have heard of some Lodges holding membership drives where they go out looking for new members. This appears to be contrary to everything I was ever told about Freemasonry, but those decisions were likely made by people with infinitely more understanding about it than I.

Once you ask to join, a painless vetting process begins, culminating in an eventual vote by the body. It is an ancient a democratic process as ever there was one and incidentally, where the term being "black-balled" derived from. (Black balls are extremely rare. Don't sweat it.)

How terrifying are the rituals?

It's scary going into the unknown, but I can assure you that you have nothing to fear. There is no hazing involved. There is absolutely nothing offensive or compromising. There is a process which all masons must pass through, where the candidate receives the degrees that he needs to be a Master Mason. We've all done it.

There is no animal sacrifice, no drinking of blood, no pact with Satan or any of the other bizarre things you might have heard of. I can't even make a joke here because the myths associated with the initiation process are taken so seriously by way too many people. It's simply a misconception. There's nothing discomforting about it.

I know that I can go to any Masonic Temple anywhere in the world and find fellowship. I know that any Mason can come to my lodge and be greeted and treated as one of our own.

I remember my first night walking up to the lodge's front door. A man following me asked where I was headed. I pointed to the door. He nodded, clapped me on the back, and said, "You are going in the right direction."

Do you know a lot of people who are Masons?

Before I joined, I hardly knew of any. As I said, no one in my family was a Mason before me. One day I ran into a fellow police officer who was wearing a Masonic ring. I asked him if he was a Mason and I asked how hard it was to join. He gave me some of the information you see here, and before I knew it I was bathing in the blood of virgin sheep.

Just kidding.

Wanted to see if you were still paying attention.

www.BernardSchaffer.com

Bernard Schaffer is the author of multiple books that span a wide variety of genres. He has worked with famous literary figures such as Harlan Ellison, Alan Dean Foster, and Bill Thompson (the editor who discovered Stephen King and John Grisham).

Recently, he collaborated with J.A. Konrath on two books that feature Konrath's best-selling Lt. Jack Daniels characters, and ones from Schaffer's own Superbia series.

A lifelong resident of the Philadelphia area, he is the proud father of two children.

Email: Contact@BernardSchaffer.com

Twitter: @BernardSchaffer

QUALITY ASSURANCE

At Dia de los Toros Publications, our goal is to provide incredible literary value to our readers for extremely fair cost. Our commitment to professionalism extends beyond the sale of our books.

Please email us if you have found any errors with this publication (must be current-gen), and upon their verification, we will send you a special gift.

WE LOVE READER REVIEWS

Thank You for Your Purchase. Please know how important reviews are to our publishing company, which dedicates itself to providing quality and innovation to its discerning readership. Your continued support means the world to us.

WE LOVE KINDLE READERS

All Dia de los Toros Publications are available on Kindle, but more importantly, they are all enrolled in the KINDLE PRIME and KINDLE UNLIMITED programs.

Kindle Unlimited users can get every single Bernard Schaffer title, or Chase Carroway title, completely free.

Thank you for your support of independent publishing!

Also Available from Bernard Schaffer

Superbia 1

Superbia 2

Superbia 3

Superbia: Down to Zero

Cheese Wrestling

Snake Wine

Way of the Warrior

Way of the Warrior 2

Guns of Seneca 6

Old-Time Lawmen

Magnificent Guns of Seneca 6

Immaculate Killers

Grendel Unit 1: Bad Day at Kor-Wa

Grendel Unit 2: Ignition Sequence

Grendel Unit 3: Fight the Power

Grendel Unit 4: Any Means Necessary

Grendel Unit 5: Automatic for the People

Grendel Unit and Far From Home: Sun Hammer 1 + 2

Return Fire 1 (Confederation Reborn)

Return Fire 2 (Confederation Reborn)

Return Fire 3 (Confederation Reborn)

A Brightly Flickering Flame (Confederation Reborn)

Fool's Gambit (Confederation Reborn)

Whitechapel: The Final Stand of Sherlock Holmes

Whitechapel: The Final Stand of Sherlock Holmes (Gentleman's Edition)

The Girl from Tenerife

Women and Other Monsters

Overdogs

Agent Omega: You Only Live Forever

Thirsty Blade

The Manifesto of Independent Writing and Publishing

Tiny Dragons 1

Tiny Dragons 2

Saokata (Episode One)

Also available: Billionaire's Apprentice, as Chase Carroway

Women and Other Monsters

Overdogs

Agent Omega: You Only Live Forever

Thirsty Blade

The Manifesto of Independent Writing and Publishing

Tiny Dragons 1

Tiny Dragons 2

Saokata (Episode One)

Also available: Billionaire's Apprentice, as Chase Carroway

Copyright 2011 Bernard Schaffer

All rights reserved. This book is a non-fiction work based on the author's personal views and do not reflect any agency or other entity.

Printed in Germany
by Amazon Distribution
GmbH, Leipzig